If My people, who are _____ _____, _____ them-selves and pray and seek My face, and turn from their wicked ways, then will I hear from Heaven and will forgive their sin and will heal their land.

That was the watchword for the first gathering. It is the watchword for this one.

If My people — those who love Me, as I love them — will humble themselves, then it will not be necessary for Me to humble them.

If they will pray — from the depths of their heart, wanting to hear Me and not themselves — then I will hear them.

If they will seek My face — not glory, not crowns, not celebration, just My face — then they shall see Me.

If they will turn from their wicked ways — the public ones they know displease Me, and the secret ones they will not even discuss with Me — then will I forgive their sin. But I cannot forgive that which is not repented of. And I will no longer condone behavior I have tolerated until now. My patience does have an end, and that end has come. You have been expecting it. Now it is here.

Each of you must allow Me to search the darkest corners of your heart. You must ask My forgiveness for every sin that I reveal to you, and I will reveal them all. If you do this in absolute contrition, I will forgive you and cleanse you with the Blood of the Lamb, whiter than snow. And you will accept My forgiveness and My Blood-washing, and go and sin no more.

Then you must ask Me if you are holding anyone in unforgiveness. I will show you. And I will tell you what you must do to be reconciled.

Only in this way will My Body be healed.

And only in this way will I heal your land.

THE
LAST
AWAKENING

A CALL TO REPENTANCE

DAVID MANUEL

McDougal Publishing is a ministry of The McDougal Foundation, Inc., a Maryland nonprofit corporation dedicated to spreading the Gospel of the Lord Jesus Christ to as many people as possible in the shortest time possible.

Published by:
McDougal Publishing
P.O. Box 3595
Hagerstown, MD 21742-3595
www.mcdougalpublishing.com

ISBN 1-58158-082-7

Printed in the United States of America
For Worldwide Distribution

About this book...

As an editor at Doubleday, I detested instant books. And after starting to write in 1973, I vowed that I would never do one. (I had yet to learn that in God's Kingdom it was unwise to say never.)

What is happening in America today — specifically, what God is doing to counteract what is happening — needs to be told by everyone who can write or broadcast or preach, as fast and as far as possible!

For what He is doing is Revival — with a big R. The thing we've read about, longed and prayed for, and almost given up ever seeing in our lifetimes, is happening. It's begun!

Most of us have been unaware of it. Dozing in our easy chairs or in our comfortable pews, we have bemoaned the rapidly gathering darkness without seeing the flashes of light and glory of God's handiwork.

There is an awakening coming, on the scale of the First Great Awakening and the Second. It may be presumptuous to call it the last awakening. It may be more presumptuous to assume there is no end to God's patience.

When I prayed about the title of this book, and how it applied to America For Jesus, this was what I heard in my heart:

It is the last opportunity I will afford My people to humble themselves and pray and seek My face and turn from their wicked ways. If they do, if they repent and are reconciled with one another, then will I hear them. Then will My body be healed. And then will I heal their land. But only then.

To

the unnamed heroes

of the

Royal Air Force
(Colorado Springs squadron)

CONTENTS

And do this,
knowing the time,
that now it is high time
to awake out of sleep;
for now our salvation is nearer
than when we first believed.

Romans 13:11, NKJ

1

THE PINE FOREST

Revival. The word was shrouded in holy mystery. I knew what it meant. I had written about revivals. Not the small revivals that might transform a church for a season. The great ones that could shake a nation — and did.

The Great Awakening, which swept through the Colonies in the middle of the eighteenth century, played a key role in the founding of America as described in *The Light and the Glory.* The Second Great Awakening (covered in *From Sea to Shining Sea*) combined with the Great Revival in the West, which had seen the entire state of Kentucky fall under the spell of God. That one had opened the nineteenth century, and the Finney Revival had been a continuation of it, a new wave.

In the fall of 1857, the Men's Prayer Revival (chapter 39 in *Sounding Forth the Trumpet*) spread throughout the North and the South and carried on into the Civil War, inspiring massive revivals in both Union and Confederate ranks. It endured and spread, to the point that some historians referred to it as the Third Great Awakening.

But there had not been a nation-shaking move of God in more than a century. To be sure, we did have the Azusa Street Revival in 1906, which introduced the Pentecostal Movement into America. And in the late 1960's the Charismatic Renewal swept many surprised citizens (including myself) into the Kingdom. Both movements had continued, but their fervor had subsided. They had grown comfortable and complacent — hardly nation-shaking.

An increasing number of us became convinced we were due for a new move of God. Overdue. We knew the prerequisites: Sincere, earnest, sustained prayer for revival. And repentance — of the search-me-O-God-and-cleanse-me-of-my-sins variety, the kind that gets *everything* and leaves you shaky but clean, as if you'd been scoured out with a divine Brillo pad.

There also needed to be reconciliation. The Body of Christ was so fractured, it scarcely resembled a body at all.

In 1977 at the Charismatic Convention in Kansas City, God the Father had spoken to forty-five thousand penitents in Arrowhead Stadium, in a word shared by Ralph Martin.

Mourn and weep,
  for the body of My Son is broken.
Mourn and weep,
  for the body of My Son is broken.
Come before Me with broken hearts and contrite spirits,
  for the body of My Son is broken.
Come before Me with sackcloth and ashes.
Come before Me with tears and mourning,
  for the body of My Son is broken.

I would have made you one new man,
  but the body of My Son is broken.
I would have made you a light on a mountaintop,
  a city glorious and splendorous
  that all the world would have seen,
  but the body of My Son is broken.

The light is dim, My people are scattered,
  the body of My Son is broken.

I gave all I had in the body and blood of My Son;
  it spilled on the earth;
  the body of My Son is broken.
Turn from the sins of your fathers
  and walk in the ways of My Son.
Return to the plan of your Father,
  return to the purpose of your God;
  the body of My Son is broken.
Mourning and weeping,
  for the body of My Son is broken.

By the end of that word, we *were* weeping. On our knees, all of us. We could see His Son's broken body on the cross. And we were overwhelmed by the conviction that it was our sins that had put Him there. We repented. And were then given to see that corporately we had kept His Body broken, with our jealousy and strife, our competition and distrust.

We begged His forgiveness — and received it. And that night we went on into resurrection joy. None of us who were there would ever forget it!

But...His Body was even more broken now. And we cared even less now. We claimed to want revival. Some of us had been praying for it for years. But if repentance and reconciliation were its cost, then the price was more than we cared to pay.

Well, then if we would not gather in one spirit and one accord at the foot of His cross, forgetting our divisions as we gazed up at His face, then His Father might, in His infinite love for us, allow circumstances to befall us that would bring us there.

There were, however, the tiniest inklings that what we had so long hoped and prayed for, might be about to happen.

Last summer, at the annual convention of the End-Time Handmaidens and Servants in Boston, their leader, Gwen Shaw, prayed for revival — the Great Awakening kind.

As she did, the Lord spoke to my heart:

For I shall come as a thief in the night, quietly, unexpectedly, entering before the householder knows I am there. And I shall come as an underground fire in a pine forest, smoldering unsuspected, spreading far and wide, ready to explode in an instant into a fire that consumes all and cannot be quenched.

I demand your heart. I do not call it. I demand it. The time for entreating is over. The time for discovery is at hand. Discover the depths of My power. Discover the extent of My reach. Now.

I am ready to move. Are you ready to move with Me? If you are, then call upon Me to search your heart and bring to light for My cleansing and My Blood-washing, any iniquity that lingers there — that you might go and sin no more. For I would have you a shining, pure instrument of My revival.

Will you join Me? Give up what I have called you to give up. Reconcile where I have called you to reconcile. Forgive what I have called you to forgive. And then rely on Me, trust Me, and forgive and forget and go on. For the time of revival is now. Not next year. Not next week. Now.

Be free. Be ready. Be Mine. Now.

2

SHAKE OFF DULL SLOTH

I had no intention of getting involved in the same-sex marriage debacle up in Boston. I did not have a dog in that fight.

The Supreme Judicial Court (SJC) of Massachusetts had decreed that as of May 17, couples of the same sex could legally marry in this state. They had picked that date, the fiftieth anniversary of the U.S. Supreme Court ruling that ended segregation, to tie their decision to the African-American struggle for civil rights.

Anticipating a strong negative reaction among the people of Massachusetts (thirty-eight states had recently passed Defense of Marriage Acts to prevent this very thing from happening), the SJC did their best to make their ruling people-proof. Not even amending the state's constitution could alter what they had done; all it could do was force the issue onto the ballot in a referendum in 2006. By then, thousands of same-sex couples would be married.

As expected, a groundswell of opposition arose. People called their state senators and representatives, and sent letters and e-mails, demanding to know what gave these justices the right to impose a law on the rest of us that favored a tiny minority (2% of the national population). They complained of judicial tyranny, pointing out that the justices were appointed, not elected, and that the vote was far from unanimous. They'd split, four to three.

The state's legislators, finding that they had a rather large Bengal by the tail and facing running for reelection in the fall, hastily convened a constitutional convention to get their own amendment in place.

Knowing that the same-sex side would field an impressive demonstration during the deliberations, a few concerned pastors and prayer warriors in the Boston area wondered if there ought not be a counterdemonstration. Somebody ought to do something to show the state — and the world — that not everyone agreed with what the SJC had done.

"Somebody" turned out to be nobody but themselves — and God. When these pastors met and prayed, they felt God was calling them to bestir themselves. Naming themselves the Coalition for Marriage, they called for volunteers to be part of a counterdemonstration. One of them called me.

I tried to be gracious as I turned them down. But they did not turn down that easily, reminding me that I'd spoken several times in the Boston area in the past year, usually in the company of my coauthor on *The Light and the Glory*, Peter Marshall. We had recalled the original vision that had brought the United States into being, and that had sustained the fledgling nation through the dark night of its soul — the winter of Valley Forge. Would I not join them now? Was it not time to return America to the spiritual origins we had described and dramatized?

But I recoiled at the prospect of getting involved in a street demonstration. And I had a good reason not to: I was hard at work on *Once Upon a Prayer*, a little book to help people dialogue with God. While I greatly admired Catholic friends like Father Mike Scanlon and Father John Randall who endured national opprobrium and even jail for acting on their antiabortion convictions, I admired them from afar. I *had* prayed for them — wasn't that enough?

Still, my spirit would not let it go. So finally I practiced what I'd been preaching and now writing about. I asked God what He wanted me to do.

It's dangerous to open that kind of dialogue with Him. What if He tells you what you really don't want to hear? Then what? Best not to ask Him.

But we'd been too far down the road, He and I, for me to pull that kind of stuff with Him. So I opened my mind — and my heart — to what He might say on the subject.

He reminded me of the afternoon I had heard the prophetic word Dutch Sheets had brought in Providence, Rhode Island, the previous April. I'd listened to a tape of that meeting, driving home from leading a listening-to-God workshop at My Father's House retreat center in Connecticut. I practically had to pull the car over to the side of the road and stop. Not since reading *The Cross and the Switchblade* had anything I'd read or heard had such an impact. Dutch Sheets was saying that God was on the verge of bringing revival to New England.

That was incredible on the face of it! Traveling evangelists routinely skipped the northeast corner of the country, rather than attempt to till the soil there — and with good reason. Having lived in New England for thirty-three years, I knew firsthand that harder, rockier soil was not to be found.

And yet, as I listened to Dutch, I *knew* it was true. The knowing was not intellectual; it was intuitive. God was about to bring revival; it was only a matter of time. A very short time.

Recalling that now, I surrendered. I would go. Perhaps cover it for one of the magazines I once wrote for years before. Then I sensed He wanted me to go not just as an observer, but as a participant. Moreover, He wanted me to fast for three days beforehand, as others were, as a means of spiritual preparation.

Fast? For a demonstration? That seemed a bit extreme, so I skipped it. (He ought to be grateful I was going at all.)

On the morning of the constitutional convention, Beacon Hill was a war zone — albeit a cheerful one. Placards,

T-shirts, banners, marchers and chanters were everywhere. To the surprise of the same-sex demonstrators, there were counter-demonstrators — about half as many, but just as enthusiastic. The police, trying to keep demonstrators out of the street and the sidewalks passable, were aware of the potential for ugly confrontation. But as both sides knew there was little chance of reaching their opponents with rhetoric, they left each other alone.

The Coalition side knew they were called to love their enemies, and in this case, with a warm sun reflecting off the statehouse's golden dome, it was not that hard. Most of the other side's demonstrators were not actually practicing an alternate lifestyle, but were there out of sympathy for the same-sex cause. Their parents may have marched with Martin Luther King or sat with Rosa Parks, and they were not about to miss out on what might be their generation's one chance to become involved with the civil rights struggle.

Except it was *not* a civil rights issue at all. In the words of preacher/historian Peter Marshall, "The Bible makes it crystal clear in Genesis that marriage is primarily for the procreation of the human race. The same-sex agenda is, therefore, a direct rejection of God's design, and a conscious and deliberate rejection of His authority."

Bishop Gilbert Thompson, leader of the Black Ministerial Alliance of Greater Boston, echoed the sentiments of African-American pastors throughout the country who objected vehemently to the same-sex side's attempt to ride on the backs of blacks. "It is not a matter of rights, but of *righteousness*. A moral wrong is *not* a civil right." In truth, it was hard to think of them as oppressed — many being among the richest Americans, and certainly among the best-educated.

Now, as we mingled under balmy skies with the sun reflecting off the golden dome of the statehouse, I smiled and shook my head. The Coalition side had the harmless-as-doves part down pretty well, but were way behind the curve on the wise-as-serpents part. They were consistently outmaneuvered in the designated demonstration areas, outside and inside. Somehow the same-sex side had managed to get into the building before it opened, and had packed out the visitors' gallery. As a secular journalist wryly observed, "You people came expecting to play checkers; they've been playing chess for thirty years!"

At the end of a long day, the legislators arrived at a compromise amendment. It stated that in Massachusetts, marriage would continue to be between one man and one woman. But the state would also recognize that two people of the same sex could enter into a "civil union." No one knew exactly what that was, but they assured one another it would have the same legal stature as marriage, with all the rights and privileges pertaining thereto. This, it was hoped, would satisfy everyone.

It satisfied no one. The Coalition side wanted the questions of same-sex marriage and civil union put to the voters separately. The same-sex side did not want to settle for anything less than marriage. It was the prize being withheld from them, the one that would finally force society to accept them as not only equal, but normal. They determined to defeat *any* amendment. If they were successful, the SJC ruling would stand.

Deadlocked, the worn-out legislators agreed to try again, a month later. And to our surprise, the secular media pronounced the placard-duel a draw.

For me, the highlight of the day occurred just before sundown out on the Common. There, in flowing ceremonial robes stood a big man with a big smile. He was easily the most striking figure in view, on a day that had seen more than its share of colorful characters. This was Bishop Patrick Mnuokebe from Nigeria. I asked him how he happened to be there.

He said that he'd spent the first five days of January in his prayer closet, to see what assignment God would have for him in the new year. It was hard to imagine anything measuring up to the previous year's, when he'd hosted Reinhard Bonnke's mission to his country.

On the last day of his vigil, God spoke to him. *I want you to go to Massachusetts.*

"But, Father, I've never been there! I do not know anyone there."

I know many. I will introduce you.

"But where in Massachusetts? And why?"

To Boston. I want you to encourage My servants there, for I am about to bring them revival.

I did not feel particularly encouraged as I walked down from Beacon Hill late in the evening. On the contrary, I could not remember feeling so discouraged. It was more than fatigue; I felt totally wiped out. What was I even *doing* there? I was an old bookwriter, not a young news reporter. (The kids at the fancy notebook computers in the press area were half my age — or younger.)

And this was not my fight. The same-sex side was going to win eventually, anyway. The tide was running in their favor. This country might have been conceived as one nation under God. He might even have given it to our forefathers in response to their prayers. But it was about to pass into the hands of those who preferred that He stay out of their affairs. And who were we, to think we could stop it? We pathetic few — a handful, attempting to shovel sand in the path of the incoming inevitable.

If not you, who? came the thought.

Not the Church. Mainline Protestant denominations were already ordaining same-sex advocates, while the Catholic Church, long a bastion of family values, was caught in a nightmare from which there seemed to be no awakening. As for the Evangelical and Charismatic Churches, they were too divided by jealousy and preoccupied with their interior programs ever to come together in a common cause — a cause which most, like me, considered already lost.

Feeling defeated, I had barely enough strength to get into my car and drive the two hours to my home on Cape Cod.

3

Once More Into the Breach

In my quiet time the following morning, God rebuked me. Had He not called me to fast in preparation? He had. Had I done so? No. I had decided it was not necessary.

Then He pointed out that it *was* my fight. It was the fight of every concerned believer who could be roused from their slumber and called to take action. He had intended it to wake me up to what was happening to the country. Only I had shrugged it off and had tried to get back to sleep as quickly as possible.

But a month later, it was a different story. I did fast and pray for three days before going back up to Beacon Hill. Because now I understood that the battle was going to be waged in the heavenlies, between principalities and powers, as well as down on Beacon Street and inside the statehouse. And the day went much better. I did twice as much — and was half as tired.

Out front, the placard battle was not as amicable as it had been before. Both sides now realized how much was at stake. So did America. Media trucks from every major network were bumper-to-bumper along the curb, their satellite antenna poles thrusting into the sky like church spires.

Inside, the din from the demonstration area reverberated

off the marble walls and floor. It was painful and deafening. "What do we want? *Justice!* When do we want it? *Now!"*

The Coalition side was again outnumbered, though not as heavily as before. And they had a great hidden weapon: prayer. Down in the basement, they had access to a committee room which we nicknamed "the furnace," and there they gathered for prayer. Some stayed all day; others repaired there from time to time, to get their batteries recharged. There weren't that many in the room — never more than a hundred; sometimes only a couple of dozen. But God was not interested in numbers; He was looking into hearts, to see if they possessed the resolve to persevere.

Late in the afternoon, I plunged once more into the ear-splitting roar of the demonstration area. Someone likened it to what must have greeted the Christians as they entered the Coliseum. Or what David heard as he went down into the valley to face Goliath. And it was combative now. Whenever the Coalition side cried, "One man, one woman!" the other side countered with, "*Two* men! *Two* women!"

In their midst was the leader of the Hispanic churches in the Boston area, Pastor Roberto Miranda. He stood like a rock, immovable, as he had all day long, surrounded by his Lion of Judah parishioners. I asked him why they were there.

"American missionaries came to our lands long ago, converting our parents and our grandparents. How can we stay inside the safe walls of our churches? America needs us! Now is the time for us to give back, for all that has been given to us!"

As the day wore on, the warriors down in the furnace wore out, often lapsing into silent prayer. Paul Jehle, pastor of the New Testament Church in Plymouth, put things in perspective: "How this vote goes is not the real issue here. God in His sovereignty is training the Christian community in how to handle conflict. But instead of just judging them for wanting to marry, we need to repent for where we've fallen short in our own marriages. What example have *we* set for the world? They see our hypocrisy and inconsistency. Only through our brokenness and repentance can we expect society to change."

Late in the afternoon, the exhausted legislators were ready to take the final vote. The same-sex side was confident they had the necessary ninety-seven votes to defeat the amendment.

But now the legislators would be voting their conscience. No more posturing or maneuvering or trying to please — now they would vote for what they thought was right.

When word reached the furnace that the final vote was about to take place, weary warriors who moments before had been too tired to move were now walking and leaping and praising God!

When the vote was tallied, the amendment had won — by five votes.

The same-sex side was devastated, but far from defeated. Half an hour after the last gavel had fallen and the legislature had adjourned, they held a rally in the statehouse for all their demonstrators and volunteers — more than two thousand. They were addressed by some of the most outspoken legislators who had gone to bat for them.

"All right," said one, "we did not get all we wanted. Civil union is like saying, 'Rosa, come to the middle of the bus!'"

Another said, "We're so close! Five people we were counting on switched their votes. But we're almost there! We've made it to third base! Now bring us home!" A fierce and thunderous yell echoed off the walls.

As I walked down Beacon Hill, I thought about what I had just witnessed. That was not a pep rally. It was a war rally, and the war was gathering momentum.

But so was the awakening it had stirred.

4

Only the Beginning

I cannot remember now what I was calling my friend David Mainse in Canada about on that warm and sunny day in early September 2001. It may have been about the fund-raising bike tour I was organizing in Ottawa and Montreal later in the month.

Waiting for the call to go through, I enjoyed the view from my lighthouse office. It was uncommonly clear that morning. The Provincetown tower, nineteen miles to the north, was easily visible to the naked eye, while a north-west wind spread a lace of whitecaps over Cape Cod Bay.

David's secretary, Valerie Battaglia, came on and told me he was hosting on the set of *100 Huntley Street*, which was going live across Canada. "But don't send any more planes into buildings, eh?"

"What are you talking about?"

"A plane from Boston just ran into the Twin Towers."

"What?!" I paused. "Tell me you're kidding."

"I'm not."

I hung up and ran downstairs and into the living room and turned on the television. It was on every channel.

My mind was stuck in denial. This can't be happening. Any moment now, the person doing the Orson Welles thing is going to announce it's all a hoax. Sick. Weird. But not real.

Except it was. I felt like throwing up, and could not take my eyes off the screen. Oh, dear God…I sat down, numb, unable to turn away, as the first building came down, and then the second. Those incredible firemen and policemen!

Later, I got on the Internet to see if there was anything there that had not been carried by the networks. There was. A wire service reporter had taken a photo of the smoke billowing from one of the collapsing towers. In it was a clearly visible face, horned and contorted with glee. I stared at it and shook my head; the enemy could not resist signing his handiwork.

The world as we knew it, changed forever that morning. The biggest shock, after the act of terror itself, was that there were people out there who hated Americans so much that they were willing to sacrifice their own lives to kill as many of us as possible.

Until that realization seeped in, we had thought of ourselves abroad as essentially likeable. Gauche at times, perhaps, and insensitive, but well-meaning, with good hearts and ready to help — the Yank in a helmet, riding on a tank into Paris and tossing the little boy a pack of chewing gum.

Two generations later we were still the good guys, the ones who had faced down Communism until it imploded, and then helped the Eastern Bloc countries come out into the light. We were the ones who guaranteed the safety of the free world. *Pax Americana*. The innocents abroad may have grown up and turned out to be not so innocent after all, but we were still decent, still motivated by wanting to do the right thing.

As a journalist I'd been in Bosnia during the war there and immediately afterward, chronicling the work of God's hand as the country emerged from its nightmare. I saw close-up just how dark men's hatred could become, and what they were capable of, when they had absolute power and no restraint. Whatever America may have done in the world, we were not like that. Not nearly.

Except in the eyes of Islamic fundamentalists, we were. The Ayatollah Khomeini had called us the great Satan, and his successors had confirmed it. Any people who offered assistance to the Jews had sentenced themselves to death in the jihad, the holy war between Islam and infidels that would surely come.

The Islamic extremists' hatred of America was as implacable as their hatred of Israel, and now they had shown us what they could do. They even convinced themselves that the Jews had destroyed the towers to make the Muslims look bad. Ridiculous? Half the Arab world believed it.

Our illusions — that we were loved, that our good deeds were appreciated, that we were impervious behind the walls of Fortress America, that we could live free from fear — came down in a great cloud of dust that morning. Nothing would ever be the same again.

For a few weeks after 9/11, the mind-numbing horror of it brought Americans together. We cared for one another, like I could just barely remember the grown-ups doing during World War II. We were in this together. We were proud of our new president and that wonderful mayor, and could not express enough sorrow and gratitude for those in New York who had fallen in the line of duty. We became more appreciative of our own police and firemen who, God forbid, might someday be required to make the same sacrifice.

But gradually our lives and our self-centeredness returned to normal. And with the exception of the occasional orange alert, the unthinkable once again became the unthought-about.

One thing *was* different, though, and that was the rate of moral decline. It seemed that after 9/11, it had accelerated. Things that were unthinkable a generation ago were accepted as commonplace today. What things? There was no need to preach to the choir. Anyone with eyes to see and ears to hear could make their own litany of the appalling and the deplorable.

Worst of all, we sensed it was only the beginning. We

had seen that the hatred of those determined to destroy us was insatiable. It was satanic. And they would not rest until they had brought us to our knees.

Unfortunately for them, that was not where we were the weakest. That was, in fact, where we found our greatest strength — praying to the One who loved us.

For there were two sides to the story that was just beginning: the dark side, which we had just witnessed, and the side of blinding light, which was about to dawn.

One of the first rays to pierce the gloom over America came on Ash Wednesday with the release of *The Passion of the Christ*.

No movie had ever been attacked so viciously before it even previewed. And there was a whiff of sulfur in some of the commentary. How dare they make a movie of Jesus suffering! Of His Blood being shed! No one will go to see it! Mel Gibson is going to lose his shirt! And he deserves to, for refusing to compromise. He'll never work in movies again!

I saw the film two days prior to its release, in the company of a thousand Baptists and Methodists. With the opening scenes, my one apprehension was allayed. The artistic quality — the cinematography, the sound, the acting, the directing — was nothing short of superb. The film's aesthetic values were as high as in any movie I'd seen. Were it not so controversial, it would be up for Academy Awards in every category.

And then *The Passion* took me over. This was not a movie you watched; it was a movie you experienced.

Was it too bloody? Absolutely! Satan hated Jesus and would inflict as much pain on Him as he possibly could!

Was the violence excessive, beyond what actually happened? Not from what I had read of the times. And not from what my heart told me.

Was it anti-Semitic? No. The religious leaders who had Jesus executed, did so to protect what was left of their fast-eroding power base. In three years of ministry, He had become more popular than all of them combined. In three more years, they would be gone. So He had to go. They were Jews, but so was Jesus.

The Roman soldiers showed greater cruelty — but no more than other men given that kind of power with no restraint or accountability. They hated being stuck in Palestine, and now here, delivered into their hands, was a man who some of those wretched Jews claimed was their king...

Mel Gibson said it best: The Jews didn't kill Christ; we did.

Coming out of the theater, I was numb. I realized that nothing I had ever seen or read, not even the Bible itself, had made me so grateful for what Jesus went through for my sake. Now I knew. And I sensed I would never forget.

No other movie had ever impacted me like that. The only one to even come close was *Schindler's List.* When I came out of that one, my first thought was that I wished everyone in America would see it. After this one, I wanted everyone in the world to see it. (And perhaps they will; it's well on its way to becoming the most-seen movie of all time.)

It was definitely a polarizing movie, but these were polarizing times. For that reason, I thought everyone who believed Jesus was the Son of God ought to see it. The time was coming when we would be tempted to deny Him. *The Passion* would remind us of the price He had paid — for each of us.

5

The House Is on Fire!

The flight attendant's voice came over the intercom. "Please return your tray tables and seatbacks to their upright position."

As the plane settled into its final approach to Norfolk, I looked at the houses passing beneath us. It was a warm June Sunday; people who had pools were taking advantage of them.

This trip was still a little hard to believe. In a few minutes I would be met by John Gimenez, whom I'd not seen in twenty-four years. I smiled at the prospect and closed my eyes. What an adventure we'd had!

John had been in his late forties then, pastor of the Rock Church in Virginia Beach. A tough Puerto Rican who had come out of the street culture, he'd been born again and filled with the Spirit of God. Now he was an on-fire preacher and evangelist with a big and growing church — and a huge assignment from God: to call the nation to a prayer rally in the spring of 1980, on the Mall in Washington D.C.

Nothing like it had ever been attempted before. Indeed, it was such a staggering undertaking that I was led to write a book about it, much as I had about the Charismatic Conference in Kansas City three years before. "Washington For

Jesus" would break new ground on many levels, the most important being that it would be the first time Evangelicals and Charismatics had ever worked together for a common purpose.

John had persuaded Pat Robertson and Bill Bright to co-chair the event, and while there were some wrinkles prior to the event, they were ironed out. Everyone — Charismatic and Evangelical, Protestant and Catholic, black and white, young and old — knew God wanted it to go His way. He had given John the vision, and the rest of us had caught it. Now He had gathered us from the east and the west, the north and the south. It was up to us to set aside whatever separated us and let Him blend us together into one spirit and one accord. We prayed He would.

He did.

The night before, there was a youth rally at RFK Stadium, so naturally we stayed up way later than we should have. And then, too excited to sleep, we went to the Mall two hours before sunrise and found thousands of silhouetted forms, praying, dozing, waiting.

Finally the dawn came — behind lowering clouds. Local meteorologists had promised torrential rain. But this was God's parade! We refused to believe He would allow rain to dampen it. We asked Him not to, and He complied.

Scarcely had we begun when the sun broke through and stayed out all day. There was a parade down Constitution Avenue with contingents from every state. There were well-known speakers and little-known speakers. But mostly there were smiles. We were glad to be there and sensed we were part of history being made.

At the high-water mark, some three hundred fifty thousand praying believers were gathered on the Mall. (Though later estimates would put that figure much higher, that was the maximum the chief of the Park Service would give me.) And when we were done, Youth With A Mission policed the entire area, leaving the Mall cleaner than when we had first arrived.

Afterwards, we sensed God was well pleased, and that our combined prayers had broken something in the heavenlies.

And now, in the fall of 2004, we were going to do it again.

A month earlier my office phone had rung, and though I'd not heard the caller's voice in years, I recognized it. It was John Gimenez. "David, He wants us to go back."

I didn't question it. In chronicling Washington For Jesus in *The Gathering*, I'd seen close-up how careful John was to stay in God's Spirit, and how much it cost him to do the will of God when it crossed other people's wills. If he said God was calling us to the Mall again, I believed it.

"I know your heart," said my friend. "I want you in our core group."

And so now I was on this plane, flying to join him.

In 1980, we could see the desperate spiritual condition of the nation. She had needed the prayers of every single believer, and the presence of all who could possibly attend.

But how much worse was the national condition now! Back then, we could not have even imagined the state of affairs we would be facing today. Indeed, many Christians believed America was too far gone to do anything about it.

Not John. He still believed that God would keep the promise He had made in 2 Chronicles 7:14 — if we would keep our end of the bargain.

But John was acutely aware of the need for immediate action. When asked by the chairman of a committee for his assessment of the current state of things in America, he burst out, "Senator, the house is on fire!"

And now I was going to help him raise the alarm. But first I would have to satisfy my own misgivings. I'd not been at the sequels to Washington For Jesus, in 1988 and 1996. And now I was fearful that, despite John's assurances to the contrary, this gathering might somehow become no more than a performance-oriented platform event or Jesus festival.

It need not be. The first one in 1980 did have some elements of glitz and glamour, but for the most part its spirit was pure. And Promise-Keepers' "Stand in the Gap" in 1997, which I'd covered for *CrossPoint* magazine, could not have been more pure. I'd heard that The Call 2000 was pure. Would America For Jesus be? That was the first thing I needed to find out.

When John greeted me, we were both pleased to see how little the other had changed. It *was* like old times! But there was one difference. Back in January, John had suffered a massive heart attack. Originally the event, scheduled for October 22, had been a prayer rally for Hispanics, *America Para Jesucristo*. Then God had expanded John's vision. He wanted the event to be for *all* of His children.

John balked. Washington For Jesus had nearly destroyed his marriage, his family, his church. He was not about to put them all through that again. But the heart attack changed his mind. He realized that if he would give God his utmost, God would continue to extend his life. After that, it was full speed ahead.

The next morning we went up to Washington, and spent the day presenting the vision to pastors, black and white, in meetings arranged by Ruth Schofield. The presenting team was Bishop John Gimenez, his sister Anna, his son-in-law John Blanchard — and me. We did our best. They seemed to catch the vision — but we would not know for sure until the day arrived.

6

The Vision

The only thing I could bring to the table was my pen. So, working with John and Robin Blanchard, I helped write press releases and letters. As we worked together, I noted that they both operated intuitively, responding to the Spirit of God, and using each other as a sounding board. They made an effective team.

The first thing we had to do was assess the situation. America was in crisis. Not since the nation had split over slavery had there been such hostility abroad in the land. And it was becoming obvious that the divide between us was more than cultural; it was spiritual.

What could be done? Many Christians believed it was too late to do anything. They had bought what the secularists were putting out, that it was only a matter of time — a short time — before control of America's destiny passed into their hands. The best thing for believers to do was hunker down inside the walls of our churches, focus on the programs that were working, and let the world go wherever it was going in a handbasket.

But was that what God wanted?

In the beginning, His plan for America was crystal clear. We were to be a nation under Him, living with Him at the center of our daily lives, both public and private. We were to pray about everything we did, every decision we made.

We were to love Him with all our heart, soul, strength and mind. And we were to love our neighbors as much as we loved ourselves.

If we did these things, He would set us as a city on a hill, a beacon of hope to people all over the world, to draw men — and nations — to follow our example.

Not everyone had to subscribe to this vision, but we needed enough to make it happen.

In the beginning, there were more than enough. The Founding Fathers all caught on to God's plan, even those like Jefferson who had not much use for Him. Not only could they see what He had in mind, but they could get it down on paper. But scarcely had the ink dried on their Declaration, than God's plan began to be less clear, less bright.

To be sure, an army had gathered on the hills around British-occupied Boston. But they were summer soldiers, confident that they'd whip the redcoats easily, and be home long before Christmas. It would be a three-month adventure with good fellows and not too much danger — something to tell the grandkids about.

But three months became six, and then a year. And now probably another year. And who knew how many more years?

In the winter of Valley Forge, 1777-1778, many Americans had lost sight of the vision God had given them. The whole thing was a dream turned sour. There were hardships everywhere now. The British occupation force had become cruel and arrogant, with nothing but contempt for Yankee-Doodle. Harvests were left to rot in the fields, because there were no men home to bring them in.

Up and down the Eastern Seaboard and across the Appalachians, Americans increasingly chose not to think about the war that would not end. They became indifferent to what was happening at Valley Forge. When they received new requests begging for food and clothing for the men there, they might send something — but their own needs came first.

The men at Valley Forge were painfully aware that this was the prevailing attitude. They were reminded of it, each time their flour ration was cut or they had to bury a comrade who had grown too weak to stay well.

Worse, they were increasingly tempted to agree with their more comfortable compatriots. What *were* they doing here? What sense *did* it make? Did they really think they could defeat the British? Did they really believe they could break away from the most powerful nation on earth?

A few slipped away from camp in the night and went home. And then, more than a few.

Yet what of those who didn't leave? What of those who kept getting thinner and colder and sicker? What made them stay, when all reason told them to leave?

They remembered the vision. In the beginning, when it shone bright and clear, they'd been ready to fight for it and, if necessary, die for it. *And these still were.* They became the keepers of the vision, the ones entrusted with keeping it alive, when the rest of the nation had lost sight of it.

In the giant crucible of an open-hearth refinery, iron ore was heated until it was molten. All the dross and impurities that came to the surface were skimmed away. What remained was pure iron, strengthened and made malleable by the refining process.

Valley Forge was America's crucible of freedom, where the Refiner fashioned the iron instrument with which He would preserve and protect His plan for future generations. There, through the suffering and determination of a remnant who never lost the vision, He forged the nation's character.

Today, we were the remnant at Valley Forge, the ones who had not lost the vision of what God intended for America. Reason would tell us that the battle was already lost, that the outcome was inevitable, that we should hunker down inside our churches and turn our focus inward, until the Lord returned.

Reason would dictate that — but we were not reasonable people! We never were! We never will be! If we will allow the Refiner's fire to purge and purify us, then we *will* be His instrument to awaken our slumbering countrymen! Let them come and join us at Valley Forge! The soul of America is not yet lost! God promised that if we would fast and pray, seek His face, and turn from our wicked ways, He would forgive our sins and heal our land.

He keeps His promises. Will we keep ours?

The vision might have dimmed, but it had not changed. Would God now have us relinquish it? Would He have us cede the soul of America into the hands of those who care little for Him?

Or would He have us awaken to her plight and do whatever we could to save her?

Christians lamented that there was nothing that could be done, and they were right. Only God could heal our land.

But He did say He would — under certain circumstances, the ones spelled out in 2 Chronicles 7:14. *If* we would humble ourselves and pray and seek His face and turn from our wicked ways, *then* would He hear from Heaven and forgive our sins — *and heal our land.*

All across the country, those called by His name were beginning to humble themselves. (Nothing was quite so humbling as public repentance — or more conducive to reconciliation.) They had begun fasting and praying. And now, multitudes were planning to come to Washington on October 22 and gather on the Mall to seek His face together.

Would He have you be there in that number? Ask Him. If He would, then let nothing dissuade you.

We sent out that invitation, far and wide.

Later, I asked John Blanchard what working for America For Jesus had been like in the beginning.

> After the '96 event, for which Robin and I were largely responsible, I went into shellshock. When combat soldiers are subjected to sustained bombardment, they sometimes get traumatized. They kind of freeze. Nothing moves them, sometimes for years. I was like that. Even on a roller-coaster ride

in a theme park, I could not scream. I just sat there, emotionless.

The same sort of thing happened to Bishop after 1980. When you understand the price you're going to have to pay, then you have to be absolutely certain it is called for by God, part of His plan to save the nation — if we follow His guidelines.

When did he know for sure it was God?

Just after Bishop switched it from being for the Hispanics, to being for everyone. To me, that was the clearest sign that God was in this, that it was going to be His event, not ours. I needed that assurance — because you have to give your life for something like this. You'd better be absolutely certain it was God.

Also, after the '96 rally, because of the spiritual warfare you inevitably encounter after exercising spiritual leadership, it's as if your picture is put up in the post offices of hell, and every demon comes after you. You'd *better* be sure!

What confirmed it?

Right away, things started going right — things we could not possibly have planned. Noncoincidences, divine appointments, doors suddenly opening that had been closed tight. Gifts from Heaven — like Apostle Betty Peebles giving us the use of her sanctuary, Jericho City of Praise, for our leaders' meeting the night before the event on the Mall. There was no way we could have gotten an appointment with her, so we just walked in and trusted the Lord. And He gave us favor. That happened over and over.

When I got home, I asked God for a watchword for this

event. He gave it to me. And then, perhaps because the phrases had become so familiar, He provided His own amplification.

If My people, who are called by My name, will humble themselves and pray and seek My face, and turn from their wicked ways, then will I hear from Heaven and will forgive their sin and will heal their land.

That was the watchword for the first gathering. It is the watchword for this one.

If My people — those who love Me, as I love them — will humble themselves, then it will not be necessary for Me to humble them.

If they will pray — from the depths of their heart, wanting to hear Me and not themselves — then I will hear them.

If they will seek My face — not glory, not crowns, not celebration, just My face — then they shall see Me.

If they will turn from their wicked ways — the public ones they know displease Me, and the secret ones they will not even discuss with Me — then will I forgive their sin. But I cannot forgive that which is not repented of. And I will no longer condone behavior I have tolerated until now. My patience does have an end, and that end has come. You have been expecting it. Now it is here.

Each of you must allow Me to search the darkest corners of your heart. You must ask My forgiveness for every sin that I reveal to you, and I will reveal them all. If you do this in absolute contrition, I will forgive you and cleanse you with the Blood of the Lamb, whiter than snow. And you will accept My forgiveness and My Blood-washing, and go and sin no more.

Then you must ask Me if you are holding anyone in unforgiveness. I will show you. And I will tell you what you must do to be reconciled.

Only in this way will My Body be healed.

And only in this way will I heal your land.

7

Forerunner

Dutch Sheets was too kind by half. That was my assessment of the foremost prophet of revival in America, as I shifted from one foot to the other, waiting for him to finish his speaking engagement. Actually, he *had* finished, but now they were clustering around him in the afterglow, each wanting a special word from God's anointed forerunner.

Dutch and Chuck Pierce were in New Hampshire in June, of 2004, nearing the end of their assignment. God had called them to visit every one of the fifty states, to bring encouragement and enhance the expectation of those who had been praying for revival. When I'd been asked to drive Dutch to a luncheon meeting south of Boston an hour and a half away, I jumped at the chance. Though we hadn't met, he'd had quite an impact on my life.

Last year I'd listened to a tape of a message he'd just delivered in Rhode Island. He was talking about what it meant to be a forerunner. He was describing himself, but he was also describing me.

Now, however, as one more person asked him for one more private moment, all I felt was impatience. We were going to be seriously late. He was aware of that, yet he continued to give the seekers his undivided attention as they poured out their private quandaries.

And then, as I fumed, God rebuked me. He reminded

me that it was precisely this compassion which had so impressed me about David Mainse up in Canada. I'd accompanied him on his cross-country broadcasting tour, and wherever we were, he always had endless time for the people who came up to him after each broadcast. The mobile studio and other vehicles in our caravan might be pulling out to begin a four-hundred-mile trek before nightfall, but David never took his eyes off the widow who was telling him how hard her life was now, without her beloved mate. He was the most trusted man in Canada — with good reason. You could see Jesus in him.

And now God was showing me that Dutch was like that. People took advantage of him, because he would never leave any plea unanswered. And neither would Jesus.

Dutch was of medium stature, with close-cropped sandy hair, strong chin, calm eyes. He wore a beige collarless jersey and a brown sport coat. His language was rough-hewn and unadorned. Only when he taught from the Bible, gleaning fresh grains from fields that had been gone over many times, did one appreciate the strength of his intellect. How much he must see — and how little he felt compelled to share. His humility was unalloyed.

Later, I re-listened to his message of the year before that had so moved me. I share elements of it here, because it sums up what it means to be a forerunner — and gives a vision for the awakening that has now begun — the last awakening.

I love the Northeast; God has put this part of the nation in my heart. He told me we can't get what we want without you all.

Wherever I go, I find a remnant, a percentage of the Body ready to go wherever He wants us to go, and do whatever He wants us to do. And God has never required a majority of the people with Him, for Him to move. He usually starts with a smaller group, and they birth it for the rest.

I want to focus tonight on what it means to be a

forerunner. I believe that where you are in New England, God is ready to confront the religious structure. It's no revelation that there's been a great religious stronghold in this part of the nation. There is coming a very direct confrontation between the true Spirit of God and the religious spirit, and when it happens, it will be fierce. These things don't just lie down and say, "You can have it." They will try to oppose what God is endeavoring to do here. But they will lose — if you don't give up.

Because the only way you can be defeated is by default. If you refuse to back up and just accept status quo, then even in spite of failures, mistakes and even ignorance, you will win, because God will see to it. He doesn't need perfection; He doesn't need people who have it all together. He just needs people who are willing to go for it with the zeal of the Lord, who will say, "I'm not going to back up." If you have that mind-set, you'll win.

Fat chance, I thought. People in New England had been running up against that religious spirit for years, for centuries. It had never lost. Yet as he spoke, something was stirring in my heart. Maybe this time it would be different....

Have you found things heating up a bit? I've often found that that happens when this particular aspect of the kingdom of darkness, this religious spirit, feels threatened. A lot of energy is released in the spirit realm, a lot of activity to work feverishly to stop it.

New England is meant to be a forerunner region. Part of the prophetic mantle that was supposed to be in the Northeast was stolen, and you're trying to recapture it. There is no gifting that the religious spirit fights more than the prophetic. They don't mind order. They don't mind structure. They don't even mind good teaching. They'll take the good and turn it into something bad.

Good things that God has used and moved through can become entrenched in religiosity and move on into idolatry. When we look to our systems, our programs — our man-made methodology — to bring life to us, then we've moved into religious structure, and it begins to empower the demonic, not the Spirit of God.

I could sense people in his audience wincing. Had some of their worship or programs or methodology become idols? I took a breath. This was strong truth he was giving them. He chuckled.

This is going to be good, if we let it be good. God's spankings don't hurt all that bad, if we embrace what He's doing. God's correction is good! We're the ones that determine how painful it's going to be. When you resist Him, of course, it gets pretty painful. We're not going to do that tonight, but we *are* going to have to get in an intercessory role for this region. That's my calling.

I want to see revival. And if you're like me, and I think you are, I want to go all the way with this thing. And if it means confronting religious powers, we're going to go all the way. How many of you are willing to say that?

Their response was only lukewarm. He offered to pray for a few minutes, to allow those who weren't willing, to sneak out. He was kidding, but then he did pray. Fervently. For revival. Not the kind that would awaken a church. The kind that would awaken a city, a region, a nation.

Lord, we want nothing less than a great awakening! We want nothing less than all-out revival! We want the culture changed! We want government changed! We want the schools changed! We want marriages changed! We want businesses to change! We want people to be overcome by Your presence and Your power! We want it to be so strong, they can't get away from it! Everywhere they go, they find You!

Hover over this region, Lord, and pour out Your Spirit! We want it to be so strong that people begin to be delivered en masse! We don't want it to just change the atmosphere in a building; we want it to change the atmosphere outside the buildings! We want it to become so strong that they begin to get delivered, set free, filled with the Spirit, healed — everywhere, Lord! In taxis, in malls, in restaurants, in schools, in businesses — we want You to interrupt the normal activities of life with such a power and anointing that people cannot get away from it!

After each phrase the people shouted. And I had slammed the steering wheel so hard, I hurt my hand. He was describing the sort of revival that had swept the country in the eighteenth and nineteenth centuries.

We want alcoholism to be broken! We want drug addiction to be broken! We want sexual perversion to be broken! We want iniquities of the generations to be broken! We want infirmities and diseases to be broken! We want mind-sets to be broken! We want religious spirits to be broken off of us, so that we're not held back in any way! So, Lord, we want the atmosphere to change! We want an atmosphere of revival in New England! We want an atmosphere of life, of deliverance, of salvation! Help us to go all the way!

There was great cheering at this. They had caught his vision. And so had I.

Now he went to the heart of the matter, showing us two

classic examples of forerunners. He started with John the Baptist.

> "Comfort, O comfort My people, says your God." The comforting part is going to be the outcome: Jesus. The word *comfort* is the Hebrew word for *repent*. And in the New Testament, the word *repent* — *metanoia* — does not mean, "turn and go the other way". That's the *result* of repentance. It means, "think differently." John said he was there to announce change. It was time to think differently!

He turned to his Old Testament example, Elijah.

> Part of the job of forerunners is to stir things up, rock the boat, bring conflict. Everywhere that things are stuck and comfortable, change is going to bring conflict.
>
> And sometimes it's easier just to leave it alone — to not become that voice. Did you know that's what the word *tolerate* means in Revelation? Jesus said to the church there, "I have this against you, that you tolerate Jezebel." The Jezebel spirit — and it can be in men or women — always partners with the religious spirit, because the two of them together are determined to shut down the prophetic spirit, which is what the forerunner anointing flows out of.

I was reminded of the Old Lights' resistance to the New Lights, and of Lyman Beecher, a great evangelist in his day, absolutely determined to prevent Charles Finney from bringing revival into Connecticut.

> That's what this Jezebel spirit says: "You leave me alone; I'll leave you alone. Just tolerate it the way it is. It's not that bad. There are a few people

getting saved. We've got a religious structure. We've got some credibility. Things are okay."

And the prophetic anointing comes along, and says, "It was okay for yesterday. It's not bad, in and of itself. But if we stay stuck here, it is bad. If we stay here — for years — it becomes rut-ism."

And the religious spirit says, "No! Leave well enough alone!"

If you let Him, the Spirit of God will rise up in you, and say, "I don't leave well enough alone! I'm in the process of restoring all things, back to the way they're supposed to be."

When Elijah came, Jezebel confronted him. "You claim your God's in control? I'm going to come after you in the name of my gods! You're not going to leave me alone. I'm coming after you!"

Dutch paused and chuckled. I could imagine him shaking his head and smiling at what he was going to say next.

I don't know why God is leading me in this direction, but I suspect New England is headed for war.

Immediately he cautioned them.

That doesn't mean we have a confrontive, mean spirit about us when we deal with other people. It just means that when that religious spirit rises up and says, "You aren't going to change this system," we don't back away. We love people as best we can, but continue to move forward in the Lord.

He paused and continued almost sadly.

If you don't do this, you'll lose your voice. If at any point you back off, then that prophetic anointing, which is what the forerunner mantle is all about, will begin to die and you'll lose your voice. There's no middle ground here; we either oppose this and win, or we lose.

You know what Ahab called Elijah? A troubler. "Elijah, you're stirring things up. You can't leave well enough alone. Just live at peace with us. We'll leave you alone. You can have your little worship time over there. You do it your way; we'll do it ours, and everything will be fine. Just leave us alone. Why do you have to stir things up like this?"

That same Jezebel spirit rose up against John the Baptist, who confronted every stratum of the culture: the government people, the businesspeople, the military, the religious — all of them. And he told them everything had to change.

"Back off and leave us alone," Herodias and Herod warned him, "or we're going to take you out."

He didn't, and they did. But not until he had completed his forerunner assignment.

All at once I imagined loose cannons taking this as blanket permission to vent their pent-up frustrations. Perhaps Dutch sensed this, too.

I'm trying to be careful here, because you can get carnal, if you're not wise. Some people don't know how to move by the Spirit in this realm. They're prophetic enough to see what needs to change, but they're not wise enough to do it in a way that God can use. They come in with an arrogance, or they come in and want to tear things up, just to tear things up, or be different, just to be different. You can be mean-spirited about this, if you're not careful.

When I talk about stirring things up and confronting and changing things and causing trouble, I'm talking about doing it *in the realm of the Spirit*.

I'm not talking about going up to your pastor and saying, "Well, I've discerned this church is too religious. You need to change!" Or becoming so arrogant that we turn everybody off with our message.

You *are* going to have opposition, when you move in this thing. But you have to learn to deal with that and walk in love. And not get to a place where you begin to war against flesh and blood. I've seen even prophetic forerunners, when they begin to be opposed, very gradually, very subtly, come out of the Spirit and begin to confront that system on an equal plane, the flesh and blood level, human to human. When you do that, when you start strife and division, you will always lose. You have to stay in the Spirit. If we do that, we can change things.

As he drew to a close, he had a prophetic word for the forerunners of New England.

In this region, the religious spirit is the greatest enemy to what God is trying to do. You're on the path of bringing revival, and I hear the Lord saying, "You've done well. You've progressed. You've come a long way. But now you are coming up against this biggest of all strongholds."

We've got to have the forerunner mind-set and spirit about us, and enough wisdom to know what's coming and what's happening when we experience these things. So when we come up against this thing, by the Spirit of God we're going to push right on through it! We're going to get the bulldozer anointing! We're going to get the dynamite out, and it doesn't make any difference how thick the mountain is. *We're going to blow it up!*

The cheers were as great as they'd been before. He let

them go on until it was time to pray for individuals.

I turned my full attention to the road, goose bumps on my arms. As soon as I could get into my prayer journal, I asked God if Dutch was truly His forerunner, and if his message was indeed from Him. This is what came:

> *It was from Me. I am about to change things in New England. I want My churches back, and I am going to have them back. I am going to blow a new wind into My churches, and it is going to blow out the religious spirits which have held them hostage for so long. It is going to blow through every church that calls itself Mine, even yours, My son. It is going to unsettle the settled. It is going to discomfort the comfortable. It is going to shake the unshakable, move the immovable, restore the lost and forgotten, bring sight to the blind, revive the somnolent, and bring tears of joy where there were only tears of sorrow.*
>
> *Make no mistake, My son; this will not be done smoothly and in good order. This will be done riotously and in holy order. Keep your sense of humor when others seem to be losing theirs, and remember, Irish eyes are not the only eyes that are smiling.*
>
> *I am going to shake your church, and every other church that calls itself by My name, as if it were a blanket, to be aired out in the sun. I love the blanket, but it needs airing, and needs to remember that I am the one who decides how the bed should be made.*
>
> *So there will be holy wars in each church that wants to be Mine. And as My son Dutch has prophesied, there will be alarm and resistance. Where it succeeds, they will be on a boulder left behind as a mighty river sweeps past. They may congratulate themselves on having avoided that onrush, but they will soon find My Spirit, which was striving with them, has departed, and they will grow older and colder by themselves on the shore. I will still love them, but I will not be able to use them as I wanted or intended.*

8

New England Sampler

On the subject of revival in New England, one of the most clearest voices was that of Paul Jehle, pastor of the New Testament Church in Plymouth, Massachusetts. Tall, dark-haired, and dark-eyed, he had a broad smile and a wry sense of humor. And in this inlet on Cape Cod Bay where the Pilgrims came ashore four centuries before, he and his church had achieved something unusual in this day and age. They had endeared themselves to the community. They did this by cleaning up the town — literally.

As one might expect, Plymouth, "America's hometown," made a big deal out of Thanksgiving. It was *their* holiday, and they looked forward to more than a hundred thousand visitors that weekend. There was a parade, of course, in which Paul's church wanted to have a float. But it was judged too Christ-specific by the town fathers, not in keeping with the principle of separation of church and state.

After the parade, the young people of the New Testament Church cleaned up the entire parade route. The town fathers were so impressed — and grateful — that they changed their minds about allowing the church float in the following year's parade. And Paul Jehle, who was an expert historian on the Pilgrims, Puritans, and Bay Colony in general, was put in charge of the entire parade.

Did he see signs of revival?

"Ten years ago there were so few prayer groups and events and meetings happening that one could attend them all." He chuckled. "Today there're so many it would be impossible to attend them all!"

Then he grew thoughtful. "The volume of prayer has been a blessing. The conviction to pray has been a blessing. But the next significant work that God wants to do in the Body of Christ is to deepen the *quality* of prayer."

Could he amplify that?

"The most historically significant and biblically focused prayer is for God to soften our hearts and help us become more obedient to Him. And so there must be a transition — from, 'God, do this for me,' to 'God, what would You have me do for You? Transform my heart, Lord, so that my character is made into Your image.' "

Gwen Shaw had served on the mission field in mainland China for thirty-four years, before founding the End-Time Handmaidens and Servants. Based in Arkansas, she nonetheless had a great burden for New England, to the extent that she held her annual international convention in Boston last summer and looked forward to holding a regional conference there in the fall.

The first time I heard Sister Gwen preach was two years ago at the late Ruth Heflin's Pentecostal campground in Ashland, Virginia. Her gray hair was elegantly coifed, and her burgundy gown made her appear statuesque. She said something I have never forgotten: "God is a God of second chances."

One evening in the fall, by her example she taught me something else. We were at Tremont Temple in Boston, when Sister Gwen began to lead us in spiritual warfare against principalities and powers that had held sway over Boston for decades, perhaps generations. We joined her, praying in the Spirit of God, full of enthusiasm, our zeal white-hot.

But after half an hour of unbroken intercession against unseen enemies, my enthusiasm had waned, and my zeal was down to embers. I looked at her, but she gave no indication that we were nearing the end.

Finally, after nearly an hour, we felt something shift in the atmosphere. A stronghold had been broken. Now we were cheering and thanking God for the victory. And I had learned what it meant to travail in prayer. I'd actually learned it a long time ago at the beginning of the Charismatic Renewal, but I'd grown complacent. Not Sister Gwen. Old warhorses never lose their taste for battle, and never falter, once the trumpet has sounded.

On the Saturday night of her convention, her keynote speaker was Benny Hinn. He taught on the book of Acts, and then he started calling out healings. "Someone is being healed of arthritis in their hands. If that's you, stand up and claim it."

I stood up. Arthritis at the base of the thumbs was so painful at times that I had to stop writing. There may have been others who stood up; I didn't notice. I claimed it. To this day, it is in remission — though periodically the devil attempts to persuade me it has returned. I rebuke him, get friends to pray with me, and it is fine.

By the time he finished calling out healings, there were a couple of hundred of us on our feet. He had us form a line to come up on the platform, where he would pray for each of us. Slowly the line moved forward, until it came to a woman about six people ahead of me whose torso was so twisted and doubled over that not even her special steel crutches seemed to help.

I wished she was not there. It was asking too much. At best, she would go home disappointed, and possibly embittered against the whole healing ministry. I knew God did major miracles of healing. I had collaborated on the story of Rita Klaus, who had been healed out of a wheelchair after suffering from worsening multiple sclerosis for twenty-six years. But ...

Since the woman could not manage the four steps to the platform, Benny came down to her. When he put his hand on her forehead and prayed for her, she collapsed under the Spirit of God, her fall eased by two men who caught her and gently lowered her to the ground. The he had them raise her up, and he prayed for her again. Then same thing happened. And again. And again.

Then he went up on the platform and called for her to join him. She did! Without crutches! We all gasped. Then he whispered words to her that only she could hear, and prayed for her one more time with the same result as before.

They lifted her up, and he pronounced her healed. The friend who had brought her, came rushing down the aisle sobbing with joy. She said that her friend had been that way for two years, as the result of having taken wrong medication. She had been in such pain, in fact, that they had almost not come to the meeting.

The healing service was over. As we resumed our seats, I asked God to forgive the paucity of my faith.

I'd worked with Peter Marshall on different history books for thirty years, and in the process had observed him become a master historian who could hold his own with any scholarly professional. Together we had researched and described the Great Awakenings that had swept over America. Who better to ask if there was another one coming?

> There is no nationwide revival yet. We've had some local outbreaks of revival in various places, such as Pensacola, Florida, and Modesto, California — what I call revival measles. But it's not af-

fected the whole country — yet.

What did he think was holding it back?

There can be no revival until the Christians take 2 Chronicles seriously and start to put it into practice. What that scripture clearly calls for is "turning from our wicked ways." Everything hinges on it. When He sees us Christians turning from our wicked ways, He will not only forgive our sins, but heal the land as well. What He is promising in this verse is supernatural intervention to bring the nation back to Himself. But the only way that can happen is through a deeper repentance on the part of the believers.

It's an interesting commentary on our lack of repentance, how many times when I'm introduced prior to preaching, the pastor quotes 2 Chronicles and unconsciously leaves out that phrase — the most important part of the verse.

Did he have any good news?

For us Christians, the good news about that scripture is we don't have to try to change the hearts of the unbelievers. He is asking us to concentrate on getting *ourselves* changed through the power of Jesus Christ. That we *can* do. And that we *must* do, if we want to see America saved.

Shelli Baker was a five-foot-one dynamo evangelist out of Branson, Missouri, whom a friend had once described as one-third Amy Semple MacPherson, one-third Dolly Parton, and one-third Joan of Arc. She'd had a burden for revival in New England ever since leading one on the campus of the Rhode Island School of Design. To an array of talents that included preaching, singing, and painting, she had now added writing. Peter and I had contracted with her to produce a young readers' adventure series based on our history books. Knowing of her passion for revival, I asked her to e-mail me her thoughts on it.

> Prayer is not a spectator sport. The ordinary layperson cannot sit in the grandstand and wait for ministers to do their praying for them. For out of the ranks of the ordinary, God has found His extraordinary intercessors. Desperation brings revelation, and their desperation has finally led them to bypass the famous players in the arena. What's coming now is a revival led by people no one has ever heard of.

And then she spoke prophetically, regarding 2 Chronicles 7:14 and America For Jesus.

> *It is not only for My people, those who call Me Savior. It is for those who are called to serve them — to serve Me — by leading the way, My prophets, apostles, teachers, evangelists, pastors — those whom I hold responsible. If they will pray, I will hear them. I will visit them. I will instruct them and lead them into repentance and show them how to gather their minions under them, even as a mother hen would gather her chicks under her wings. And I will hover over them.*

In New England where I live, something's happening. Churches are beginning to bond. Gateway Ministries Fellowship, with some fifty churches and ministries under its wings, is an example. It is an offshoot of the super-fast-growing church, Gateway Christian Fellowship, headed by Pastor Brian Simmons who, with his wife Candice, served on the mission field in the jungles of Panama for eight years prior to being called to West Haven, Connecticut.

Brian had a special burden for the youth of the Northeast. He organized The Call New England and worked with Ché Ahn and Lou Engle to bring four hundred thousand young people to the Mall four years ago. His primary focus? Mentoring young leaders and preparing them for end-time ministry.

I asked him if he saw revival coming to New England any time soon.

"Without a doubt! In fact, the early stages of it are already here. The hunger level of the people of New England for an authentic move of God — a new awakening — and the depth of their passion to know Jesus, has never been stronger. And it's not just the people; the longing of their leaders for something beyond church as we know it, is deep and genuine."

How did he explain that?

He thought for a moment. "It's as though hundreds of churches have come to the end of themselves. They've tried everything else, and are finally realizing that it's going to take night-and-day prayer and fasting to see God's purpose fulfilled."

What was it like at Gateway?

"I attribute our growth to one thing: pursuit of the presence of God. In each of our Sunday services, we come into His presence in the beginning of our worship and stay there for at least threequarters of an hour. Soon the sanctuary is saturated with the love of God, and the Holy Spirit's presence is tangible. That's when our people often receive healing from crippling life issues."

Was there anything else that made it special?

"We cherish freedom — in allowing the people to touch God's heart and go out into the larger community, as examples of those who have been drenched by His presence."

Back to revival — was there anything he saw that made these new stirrings unusual?

"It's the youth who are getting it. In Maine, in Massachusetts, in Connecticut, even in New York and New Jersey, they think nothing of jumping into a car and driving more than a hundred miles to experience God's presence. It's exciting to them — and to us, to see their faces as they pray, and the hope in their hearts. They are going to lead the charge — and they know it!"

He warmed to his subject.

"Their faces are set like flint, and they won't be turned back! They want it fresh, real, and without a religious spirit." He paused. "My personal feeling is that somewhere soon in New England — at a prayer meeting led by youth, the Holy Spirit will fall with such signs and wonders that we'll all realize we're witnessing the beginning of the Last Great Awakening!"

9

THE NO-NAME REVIVAL

The last week in August, two leaders of the national forty-day prayer initiative called a conference of the various regional directors at the World Prayer Center in Colorado Springs. I was invited to attend.

I'd met the leaders, Ray Bringham and Tatsuo Akamine, at America For Jesus' leadership conference in Virginia Beach and was looking forward to seeing them again.

At 85, Ray Bringham was the oldest of the old warhorses. I was surprised our paths had not crossed in the early days of the Charismatic Renewal. He'd worked with David Duplessis, Bob Mumford, Dennis Bennett, Harald Bredesen, and Pat Robertson when I'd been their editor at Logos. Ray had a warm smile, blue eyes, and short gray hair, and he was always dressed in a suit.

All his life, his special burden was prayer and repentance, and in 1982 he'd lain on the floor all night, seeking God. Finally he heard Him say, "Call the leaders of the nation together to pray, and call it a prayer summit."

So he did. More than sixty responded and joined him on Prayer Mountain in Kentucky. Dr. Tom Carruth of Asbury Seminary called it the greatest corporate prayer experience of his life.

Out of it came the Prayer Summit movement, and today

Ray was president of the World Prayer Summit, based in San Marcos, California. At the beginning of the year, he had met Tatsuo Akamine, a Japanese-American youth minister with a similar burden for organizing corporate prayer and fasting for America. They joined forces, and God favored their endeavors. Well-known ministries like Focus on the Family, Campus Crusade for Christ, and Dr. D. James Kennedy's organization lent their support. A prayer initiative nicknamed Forty Days for the USA emerged — forty days of prayer and fasting for national repentance, to commence on Yom Kippur, the Jewish Day of Atonement. I asked Ray, "Why forty days?"

Nate Krupp gave me the idea back in 1992. It was how long Jesus fasted and resisted the devil in the wilderness, and how long Moses spent on Mount Sinai, when the Lord gave him the Ten Commandments.

What got you started?

I was praying in the middle of the night, when God told me to go to the National Day of Prayer in Washington, D.C. It's always the first Thursday in May. Vonette Bright started it. She got Congress to pass legislation to make it official.

I told Him, "I can't do that, Lord. I'm too old. I'm 85!" As if He had forgotten. He told me to meet with the National Prayer Committee the day before, and explain it to them. Well, I could do that, and so I went.

At their meeting the day before, I showed the head of the committee what President Abraham Lincoln had written:

"It is the duty of nations as well as of men to own their dependence upon the overruling power of God, to confess their sins and transgressions in humble sorrow yet with assured hope that genuine repentance will lead to mercy and pardon, and to recognize the sublime truth, announced in the Holy Scriptures and proven by all history: that those nations only are blessed whose God is the Lord."

When he read it, he said, "We need to repent." He got down on his knees, and so we all did, about fifty of us. And we had about an hour and a half of awesome prayer. The next day, there were five hundred people in the Senate Office Caucus Room. On their knees.

How did you and Tatsuo get together?

As soon as I got home, I got a call from someone I'd never heard of, named Tatsuo Akamine. He'd called Campus Crusade to see if they were planning a call to forty days of prayer and fasting. They weren't, but Vonette told him to call me. I had written her and Shirley Dobson to express the deep burden I had to call America to national repentance, in the form of forty days of prayer and fasting. When I told Tatsuo that, we saw that our hearts were together.

A few days later, Tatsuo came over. We were joined by Bud and Betty Miller, who'd driven over from Arizona to meet with us. They run a popular website called Bible.com. My wife Mib joined us, and when we all prayed together, Betty had tears in her eyes. She asked God, "How can I do this? We had fifty million hits last month! I'm full up to here!" He told her, nevertheless, that He wanted her to take this on.

We all drove up to Pasadena, to meet with Lou

Engle, the leader of a young people's prayer fellowship, The Cause. He said, "Tatsuo, how can we change our dates? We've already started a fifty-day fast!"

Tatsuo said, "There's no conflict. You're following God. So are we. Yours will help ours."

Beautiful! Unity in the Body. That's the way we all ought to respond to one another's calling! Then what?

I talked to Gary Bergel, the head of Intercessors For America. More unity. We agreed on calling it forty days of corporate prayer and fasting for national repentance. Gary said there were other groups planning forty-day fasts at different times, but most of them decided to tie in with us and start on Yom Kippur.

God said that in the last days the young men would see visions and the old men would dream dreams. What was he dreaming these days?

I believe we're in the first stages of the greatest revival the world has ever seen! This is clearly the most critical time in the history of our Republic. We face enemies abroad and at home, bent on destroying us and our society.

But there's now a shift. We may have turned a corner. But without repentance, revival will never happen. It's time for every man and woman who loves God to let Him search their hearts and show them where they must ask Him to forgive them and wash them in the Blood of the Lamb.

As I thought about the things Ray had told me, I was struck again by how many unknowns God was using in these various initiatives. Truly it would not be inappropriate to call it the No-Name Revival.

And the most encouraging sign of all was how the various ministries and initiatives were gladly blending with one another. No jealousy, no turf wars, no competition or saying that one calling was more important than another. What I saw was the opposite, a deferring one to another — which was so far from the way ministries used to behave towards one another.

Ray was calling for repentance and reconciliation. I used to think it was impossible but now I was witnessing it.

When someone jokingly referred to the No-Name Revival, I chuckled. It could also be called the No-Funds Revival. No honorariums, no travel expenses — if people came, it was in response to God's call, and God would have to cover their expenses. Everyone was operating on a shoestring, determined not to spend what they did not have. This, too, was a remarkable difference from times past.

I'd never heard of Tatsuo Akamine. He was young (at least to me), but there were seams of care in his face that gave witness to pain and suffering in his life. He had no base of operations, yet God had favored him mightily as he sought to gather people for the forty-day prayer initiative.

Listening to him, I began to realize something about the coming revival: It was going to be borne on the shoulders of those who could hear the voice of God and who would respond in obedience to what they heard Him ask of them. Some would be young — really young, like campus evangelist Jaeson Ma, who would be speaking later that morning. Or young at heart, like Tatsuo. (With a shock, I realized that I was no longer one of the young ones, as I had been out in Kansas City or at Washington For Jesus.)

During Tatsuo's quiet time that morning, he had received a strong word from God, which he shared with the rest of us. It was an admonition for all of us — for anyone serving Him in the coming revival:

You must spend time in My presence daily, before

you go on your way. Intimacy is everything. What I am calling you to do is not humanly possible. It goes against the grain of human reasoning and ability. That is why you must wait on Me, draw strength from Me. I will tell you what you must do.

I will open the doors for you. Do not rely upon your own understanding. I will counsel you. But I cannot, if you are not abiding in Me, and My words are not abiding in you. When you come to the end of yourself, that is where I will come in. Do not fear, do not be dismayed, for I, the Lord your God, am with you, wherever you go.

What Tatsuo had to say that morning was heard by only forty or so prayer leaders. Yet it needed to be heard by every man and woman whom God was waking up and calling to active duty. And it would be. For in that small meeting in addition to us no-namers were Dutch Sheets, Lou Engle, Bill McCartney, Eileen Fisher, and John Blanchard.

Tatsuo based what he had to say on what he had heard God speak to him, in the depths of his heart.

It's all about intimacy. It's not about a program. It's not about our great and wonderful ideas and organizing abilities. God says, *"No more of that. You are going to be utterly dependent upon Me. You cannot rely on your own strength."* And let me tell you, saints, the assignment God has given each and every one of you, in this most critical time in the history of our nation, is beyond human ability. That's the way you will know you must be *utterly* dependent upon Him, and then He will get the glory. *"Then you will know that I am the Lord, your God, and this nation will come to know that I am the Lord, their God."*

But it must begin with us — in intimacy, spending time in His presence. You can't depend on yesterday's experience. You can't go on doing good things, good ministry things. You've got to get in alignment with Him. Fresh oil, for a fresh day. Don't glory in yesterday's victory. Today there are new battles. Tomorrow will only come by what we do today. And that's why this intimacy with Almighty God is very key. *Now. I am the God of now.* You can't substitute that.

Oh, we try. We go on autopilot. That's not the same as going under the anointing. It's all about the anointing. It's all about hearing His voice saying to you, *This is the way; walk in it,* when there are myriad voices in our minds. Your voice, the voice of others, the voice of this world, the voice of Satan — then, the still, small voice."

And now he said something that resonated with my deepest understanding of the coming revival.

What God is doing now — in our nation and in the world — will be led by those individuals totally broken of their own confidence. No names! Don't worry about status. Don't worry about whether you're going to be recognized. The only thing that matters is what God sees when He looks upon you and to be obedient to His plan and His purposes.

10

Out of the Tunnel

One of the people at the Colorado Springs conference was Eileen Fisher. For thirty years she had been a teacher and leader in the prophetic. Based at the World Prayer Center under Pastor Ted Haggard and traveling extensively to hold prophetic workshops, she was slender and middle-aged with bright blond hair, and possessed of the quickest wit I'd encountered. She instantly saw the funny side of any situation and usually shared it — especially when she was making fun of herself.

Her holy humor was a gift, I realized; it sugarcoated teaching that was at times strong medicine. Eileen, for all her lightheartedness, was wise in the ways of the Spirit. I asked her what her take was on what was being said. Did it line up with what she'd perceived in her travels around America?

> We are about to experience an unprecedented move of God's glory. And this time it will be God doing something, rather than man trying to make God do something.
>
> Our nation is heading into the fullness of time, and what happens will follow Heaven's agenda, not man's. Within this move will also come a tre-

mendous fear of the Lord, which will birth wisdom in people, so they'll be able to handle this move of glory.

Many had been praying for such a move, though they might not like all of it, when they finally got what they'd been praying for.

God has had mankind on their knees for a season, to bring this move. He initiated it in the heavenlies, then put it in the heart of man, so we could walk it out on the face of the earth.

America is coming to the end of a dark tunnel. For those who prefer to stay in the dark tunnel, who feel safer there, it will still be available to them. They can live there. But there's going to be an exodus, a coming out, just like there was out of Egypt, as people come into glory.

There's also going to be grace. Grace and glory are going to walk hand in hand. And people are going to be walking hand in hand with them in this next move.

What else were we going to see?

The next move is going to see each person building their own prayer shelter. The shelter will be like a spiritual tent, and its center pole will be God's grace for that individual.

God is moving. He is confronting people with a challenge to come into a very deep and personal time of experiencing Him face-to-face in prayer.

We're moving, too. Out of this present time, where a very small percentage feel called to intercessory prayer, and neighbor depends on neighbor for their prayer support. God is calling His people to come back into the intimate garden of prayer, as depicted in the beginning of the Bible. Back then, there was no neighbor to run to. There was just Adam and Eve and God. Just man, woman, and God in the intimacy of prayer and fellowship.

God is going to put things in order, but it won't be without a fight. For He is pulling down a shaky foundation that has been built on man, and establishing a solid, unchanging foundation built on Him.

The Kingdom — on earth.

It's going to be an incredible, exciting time! Just as when salvation came to the world. It was something new, and it shook the whole earth and governments. It was prophesied in Isaiah that Jesus would carry the government of nations on His shoulders.

In advance of a great storm at sea, ships receive a signal to seek haven in a safe harbor. That's what's happening now. God is sending a clear warning signal from His heavenly lighthouse, calling all His vessels together for agreement, so they'll be able to weather the dark storm ahead.

So she was, on balance, optimistic.

Absolutely! Are we not under a time of grace just now? But true grace carries within it truth and accountability. We're leaving marshmallow faith and heading into solid faith, where people come out of the tunnel and stand on their faith. And because the Spirit of Truth shall prevail, they'll have to call sin what it is, and deal with it. The grace will be there. *Where sin is, grace abounds* [Romans 5:20].

God isn't blind, nor is He winking at America's sin. With the heart of a longing Father, He is waiting for America, His prodigal, to come home.

11

AN ELIJAH REVOLUTION

Lou Engle was the featured speaker that morning. With deep-set eyes and a pointed chin, his narrow face resembled the end of an axe. He wore a white dress shirt, and being in the forty-fifth day of a fifty-day fast, his belt was taken in to its last notch. His home was in Pasadena, but he was here to lead several hundred young people in their fast. They were The Cause — as in "Is there not a cause?" [1 Samuel 17:29].

As he got into his message, he rocked on the balls of his feet, in rhythm to what he was saying. His voice was raspy, as if he'd been speaking frequently to large crowds without benefit of amplification.

His message was full of fire, and I could see why young people were drawn to him. They liked absolutes. So did he.

God took me to the book of Malachi, and I saw how angry He was. His priests were no longer teaching the people right and wrong. It sounded just like America!

But at the end of that dire message, God said, "I am going to send something more powerful than all of this. I am going to send an Elijah revolution – a revolution so powerful it can literally break the curse off a nation, and turn the nation back. I will send the spirit of Elijah. I will turn the hearts of the fathers to their children, and the hearts of the children to their fathers."

Malachi was not the only place in the Old Testament where Lou saw discomfiting parallels between then and now.

We're living in a culture dominated by Baalworship, a Jezebel-Ahab culture. In the day of Jezebel there was temple prostitution and male prostitution. And what did God say to the Church? "I have this against you, that you tolerate the woman Jezebel who seduces my bond-servants into sexual immorality" [Revelation 2:20]. As Francis Frangipane says, this toleration in the Church is mostly inward. We may not be doing the outward works, but inwardly we are like eunuchs in Jezebel's palace. Our prayers and our preaching are like the whimpering of eunuchs who have been emasculated from their prophetic voice.

I winced, but had to admit that the Church had hardly spoken with the moral strength and clarity she would have in earlier generations – back when she was, as Lou put it, the head of society and not the tail.

The spirit of Jezebel is strong! It seeks to shut up and silence the voice of the Church. Our prophets are hiding in caves. The Antichrist spirit is raging in the land! We're witnessing a titanic clash of worldviews: One that can still call evil 'evil' and good 'good,' and another that is awash in a sea of relativity.

I cannot go the way of political correctness any longer! It is time for the trumpet to be sounded forth in the land! God is calling His prophets out of their caves! He is calling them to be heroes in a moment of crisis! Whom will you choose? Baal? Or God?

It's come to a place where Joram asks Jehu, "Have you come in peace?" And Jehu says, "How can there be any peace, as long as the sorceries and adulteries of your mother Jezebel dwell in the land?" [2 Kings 9:22].

There comes a time when there is no peace, and the zeal of God begins to consume a people. That time is now!

If we were in a stadium, we'd be on our feet, roaring! Now Lou turned to the mission of the regional prayer leaders.

In a dream, a friend saw me kneeling and heard God in an audible voice reading from Psalm 50. God, the Mighty One, arises to judge the earth. He's coming to judge this nation in covenantal judgment, to see if we can be under His covenant again. "Gather to Me My godly ones, who have made a covenant with Me by sacrifice." That's the answer! In times of darkness, gather the ones who have made a sacrificial covenant, who can still turn a nation back to God!

Gather the ones who have made a sacrificial covenant. In that instant, I understood why it was not enough to fast and pray at home; why we had to gather on the Mall on October 22, to seek His face together. Lou gave further spiritual definition to that gathering.

In 1997, Promise-Keepers put a million and a half men on the Mall. I don't think people understand how important that is. Derek Prince, in his book

Shaping History Through Prayer and Fasting, said that when men and women begin to pray and fast, God literally topples thrones. But he added that the greatest weapon of the Church is not fasting and prayer. It is collective fasting and prayer! It is Joel 2! It is Jehoshaphat! It is Esther! It is blowing the trumpet, that *everyone* joins in massive, united fasting and prayer. It is not just individuals; it is the *corporate* sound of the trumpet of the prophets that says: "We are in crisis!"

Lou had just given the credo of America For Jesus – the reason why we were going to Washington, the head of the nation.

Promise-Keepers' "Stand in the Gap" was one of the most powerful events in the history of the Church in America. I believe it closed the door of the enemy for a season. But you don't stop on that day. You must keep following the pillar of cloud and the pillar of fire.

A week later, I was looking at a picture from that event, of a man and a younger man praying. And the Spirit of God came upon me, and I said, "The hearts of the fathers are turning to the children, but the hearts of the children must turn to their fathers. And there is coming a corresponding movement of kids going to the Mall. It will be an Elijah generation – a John the Baptist, Nazirite extreme, fasting and praying generation. And when they go to the Mall, it will be a sign that America is turning back to God."

So that was how The Call began – with stadiums filled with fasting and praying young people. And three years later, the largest youth rally of them all assembled on the Mall, exactly as Lou had been shown. But as that day approached, it was not smooth, nor was it easy.

"We know Promise-Keepers, but who are you?" We ran into that often. We had dreams that no one would come. I had a recurring nightmare: I was up on the platform with four Jumbo-trons on the Mall off in the distance, and forty people showed up! I would wake up, sweating!

Lou had just articulated a private nightmare of my own – and one that I suspected had tormented the sleep of other planners of America For Jesus. I hoped our ending would turn out as happily as his has – even half as happily.

At 5:30 A.M., some estimated that two hundred thousand young people had already gathered in the night watches, to watch the sun come up. All told, twice that number came to fast and pray – not to the sound of a rock band, not to the sound of a worship team or a big preacher. God help us, we don't need personalities any more! We've got to get *God* back on the scene!

They came. It was a field of dreams, with the hearts of the children turning to their fathers.

Now he came to a topic dear to my heart.

Two things are needed for the restoration of a nation and the sustaining of it: The testimony of God's history must be maintained in the land. If the people don't know their history, they don't know where they're going. We need to recover our history for a new generation. We need to tell them the testimony.

Secondly, we need to recover the law of God. Once these two things, history and law, are knocked out, then we lose a whole generation. "There arises a generation that knew not God, nor the things that He had done" [Judges 2:10].

Having coauthored *The Light and the Glory* with Peter Marshall, I was nodding in agreement. Then he added something that had us murmuring "Amen."

We are working on history right now. We are in an unraveling of history, and to miss this moment is to miss everything! Because you can obey up to a point, but if you stop obeying, then it all shuts down. And it's been all in vain! I believe we're in that moment right now.

What did he see coming next?

Out of that prayer meeting, God began to raise up day-and-night intercession. I believe we're going to see day-and-night intercession all over the earth! God is going to raise up a house of prayer that contends with every other house! Things have got to shift. "My house shall be called a house of prayer" – not a house of programs! And if the adults don't do it, the kids are going to rise and do it!

And they *are* doing it! A young Davidic generation! They don't want to listen to sermons all day long. They want to sing and prophesy, and pray in the Father's house! And that's what they've been doing, for forty-five days. And they don't want to go home! Because something has captured their hearts. They're a new breed of fliers coming. They're going into fasting and prayer, and they're going to shake nations!

I was not exactly sure what he meant by a new breed of fliers, but I was about to find out....

12

THE ROYAL AIR FORCE

That evening, Lou and his wife Therese asked me to speak to The Cause — the young prayer warriors who had been praying night and day with him in a former warehouse on the other side of Colorado Springs.

The evening meeting at the World Prayer Center had run long; it was 10:30 when we entered a vast, high-ceilinged space filled with young and young-at-heart people, singing and praying. I felt like I'd stepped back thirty-five years, into a campus Charismatic gathering in the early days of the Jesus Movement.

The place was mostly dark, for the benefit of the kids curled up in sleeping bags, catching a few z's, so they'd be fresh on the 3:00-to-4:00 shift, or the 4:00-to-5:00. But most were up and worshiping. The ex-warehouse looked clean and scrubbed — like the smiling faces that greeted us.

I had no idea what I was going to say. In the car on the way over, all that came to me was to encourage them. God, it seemed, was well pleased with their perseverance and their enthusiasm. All He wanted me to do was assure them that He would continue to provide grace they would need with each new prayer assignment.

Lou told them who I was and asked me to give them an insight into our history that might be applicable to America's situation today. I told them about the vision-keepers at Valley Forge, whom they so resembled. The parallel was obvious; its responsibility was momentous.

I was about to leave it at that, when something else struck me. I told them that they reminded me of the Royal Air Force in the Battle of Britain. In the fall of 1940, Hitler was poised to cross the Channel and invade England. Nothing could stop him. His *Panzer Korps* had swept Europe with heart-stopping speed. His new concept of lightning war, *blitzkrieg*, had left the Free World reeling.

But before he could commit his armada to the English Channel, where they would be exposed to attack from above, he must have air supremacy. He sent the Luftwaffe to clear the skies of British fighter planes. It should take no more than a few days.

Yet day after day, as the Messerschmitts came over, Spitfires and Hurricanes rose up to meet them. The pilots in them were young — the same age as those in The Cause. Each day there were fewer defenders, until finally the British had only five serviceable aircraft left that could rise to meet the foe.

But Hitler did not know that. At that moment, he lost heart for destroying the R.A.F. and turned his wrath to devastating London and other population centers. The air wings which had been battered almost out of the skies, had a precious respite in which to recover.

Never again would Hitler come close to having an opportunity to clear the skies of Britain's defenders. Their prime minister, Winston Churchill, summed up what these courageous young pilots had done for their countrymen: "Never have so many owed so much to so few."

When Lou came forward and took the microphone, he said, "David did not know that when we began forty-five days ago, I'd called you the Royal Air Force and had even recited that Churchill quote to you."

Then he asked them to gather and pray for me. They did. More than a hundred of them, gently putting hands on me or reaching out to me. And not just for a few moments — for half an hour. Receiving God's love through them was an experience I would never forget.

13

DIVINE APPOINTMENTS

One of those who had come to Colorado Springs was John Blanchard. Tall and smooth, with an easy smile, he talked fast and thought faster. He gave new definition to the term multi-tasking. And it was a gift; he really could keep a dozen developing situations in his mind at the same time — though he did occasionally wish he had a couple of helpers with him just to do follow-up.

Most impressive — another gift — was his ability to make key decisions instantly. Like his wife Robin (John Gimenez's daughter), he decided things intuitively, never stopping to reason them out. He relied on God's Spirit to lead him.

Five weeks before America For Jesus (AFJ), I asked him how things were going, from the perspective of the most advanced of the front lines. He began with Colorado Springs.

> When we heard about the conference, it seemed we should go. Many prayer streams joined in Colorado Springs. It was a hub of intercessory prayer.
>
> From the beginning, I'd been very aware of The Call. Ché Ahn and Lou Engle had led that movement, which had seen so many young people come

to the Mall in 2000, for fervent intercession for the nation. If those two were to endorse America For Jesus...

So I put it on my heart: What if Ché Ahn and Bishop Gimenez were to join forces....

Then I discovered that Ché Ahn was scheduled to be at another conference. Very discouraging, but I didn't give up. I tried to find friends of his who might speak to him on our behalf. Finally Mike Berry called. I went over to Mike's and got on the phone with him and Ché.

I'd just seen the executive committee list. Ché Ahn was the first name after Bishop Gimenez. What had persuaded him?

I just asked him to ask God: Was America For Jesus of Him? He did. God confirmed it. "So now I'm going to have to move things in my schedule to be there."

Meeting him was another divine appointment. There were only three days in the whole month that Ché was going to be at his church in Pasadena. They happened to be the same three days that Bishop and I were going to be out there, to be on television.

Right along, my prayer had been, "Lord, make us one" [John 17:11]. We met at a steakhouse and had a long talk. He said, "We want a nameless, faceless move. Yet — whenever we promote a Call, people want to know who's going to be there. It's how someone assesses an event."

"It's how I assess an event," I admitted. "As Jim Cucuzza says, 'If someone has a name in the Body of Christ, they've probably earned it.' These men and women are trumpets that God has put in place. It's not their sin that we make them into celebrities. It's ours."

So that's how Ché agreed to serve on the board and help mobilize his network to the Mall.

What about Lou Engle?

Lou was key. When I heard he'd be speaking at the conference, that settled it; I was coming. But I didn't know he was temporarily based there, leading The Cause. At the invitation of Jaeson Ma, one of his young evangelists, I went to his meeting the night before you did. And wound up sitting next to Dutch Sheets and just behind Lou.

I invited them both to lead prayer at AFJ. Lou asked about the program, because he wanted to be involved with prayer, but not with showcasing ministries. When I explained that was Bishop's vision, he embraced it totally! Owned it! Dutch said he had a prior commitment that could not be changed, but he would try his best to get there. At which point Jaeson offered me the 3:00 A.M. prayer slot that night. I declined.

Ted Haggard was another divine appointment. Then the next morning, Eileen Fisher arranged for me to meet him, and tell him about AFJ. He said, "I know all about the event. I teach that in 1980, Washington For Jesus was what turned the nation." He said he would move some things in his schedule, but he would be there. And he would notify his churches and encourage them to come.

His churches?

The forty-three thousand churches in the North Association of Evangelicals. He's their president.

I shook my head in wonder at the doors God kept opening. America For Jesus was similar in feel to the first event, twenty-four years earlier. It had the same electricity, the same sense of building anticipation. But there was one huge difference. For the first one, the one that opened the Mall for all the other events that would follow, they had spent well over a year getting ready. It had seemed like they were pushing a giant boulder up a steep hill. They would make progress, then lose footing, and the boulder would roll back on them. It almost seemed as if God was testing them. What they did was pray and push harder, and finally by His grace, and barely in time, they got it to the top of the hill.

This time, the boulder was just as large, and the hill just as steep. But this time, God was pushing the boulder for them. Opening doors, without them even asking. Arranging appointments for them, that they never would have dreamed of. They did lose their footing occasionally, but only because they were scrambling to keep up with the boulder.

How did he feel about things now?

> We've done about all we can to get the word out, though I'm still ready to go anywhere, if there's a group who hasn't heard about it. Now, we need to do all the follow-up. And the people who still haven't made up their minds need to ask God if He wants them to be there in that number.

Any misgivings? He thought a moment.

> Everywhere we go, we're experiencing tremendous favor — opportunities and coincidental meetings that only God could have arranged. But we're also running into tremendous apathy, on the part of more than a few high-profile leaders.
>
> A lot of them have become so big they eventually become self-sufficient. They don't need anybody else, and gradually they cease to notice the needs of others. They've become religious organizations, instead of living organisms in the Body of Christ.
>
> And so, here we come with this prophetic call

from the Lord, and they say, "Well, let me see how that fits in with our calendar." If the house is on fire, you don't look to see if putting it out fits into your schedule.

All at once, he laughed.

Mind you, I don't judge. We've got a busy schedule ourselves. Still — it's like there's a veil over their eyes, so they can't see what God wants to show them.

He's calling an army for revival in America. We haven't had time to build a network, so whoever shows up — they're the network. Many are called, but few are chosen. Those who show up are the chosen.

14

SOLEMN ASSEMBLY

Whenever I talked with intercessors across the country, one name kept coming up: Gary Bergel, the head of Intercessors For America. Finally, I called him – and found someone I felt I'd known for years.

Intercessors For America (IFA) was a prayer fellowship of some seven thousand churches and pastors, committed to a day of prayer and fasting on the first Friday of each month. First Friday united prayer and fasting was the spiritual "heartbeat" of IFA, and they had been doing it for more than thirty years and were now sending out 50,000 newsletters each month to alert several times that number to national prayer concerns. In addition, they were now focusing on encouraging churches everywhere to join with them on October 10, to observe a solemn assembly. It could be in a church or in a school, in a living room or on the steps of a statehouse.

It would be for two hours, starting at 12:00 noon Eastern time. The first hour would be spent in repentance – personal, corporate, interdenominational, and interracial – and then in reconciliation. The second hour would begin with Holy Communion and would then focus on prayer – for the healing of our communities, and relational reconciliation, then for the state and the nation, and then for the world and the fulfillment of the Great Commission.

Gary explained the origin of the concept, referring me to the work of Richard Owen Roberts. It came from Joel, where God commanded His prophet to declare a holy fast and proclaim a solemn assembly [Joel 1:14, 2:15]. And as its name implied, it was a time when people gathered to examine the condition of their souls before God, to confess their sins, and to repent. A solemn assembly was a time for a people to return to their God.

I was familiar with such assemblies, from early American history. The Pilgrims and Puritans had brought droughts to an end with them. If God was withholding rain when they desperately needed it, it behooved them to find out what He might be displeased with them about.

In 1742, Jonathan Edwards wrote, "I have often said it would be a thing very desirable, and very likely to be followed with a great blessing …that there should be an agreement of all God's people in America …to keep a Day of Fasting and Prayer to God; wherein, we should all unite on the same day…sending up their cries to the same common Father for the same motives."

When I asked Gary if in his travels he saw signs of revival coming, he told me about the Boiler-Room Movement, which had come over from England. It was young people mostly, gathering for sustained 24-7 prayer, much like I'd witnessed out in Colorado Springs with Lou Engle's group, The Cause. God's intention was for His people individually and corporately to live in a state of continual revival with Him. Or to put it another way, in a state of perpetual intimacy. That, Gary explained, was His original intent: 24-7 revival, not sporadic bursts of revivalism.

What was the key?

> Every believer is to be a revival-igniter. Every believer is to be a Kingdom-bringer. Because every believer is a Christ-carrier. Our difficulty is in staying in intimate union with Christ within.

For him personally, what was the most encouraging sign?

The youth. They feel and know the same love of God and of their neighbor that I experienced in the Jesus Movement in the late 1960's and 1970's. I find their example profoundly moving – and convicting.

The more time I spend with them, the more fun I have. I can honestly say I'm having the most fun with Jesus, in both fishing for men and Kingdom-bringing, since my days as a new believer in the Jesus Movement!

Then he grew thoughtful.

I am realizing more and more, how little reaching others for Christ has to do with me, and how it has everything to do with Him. What I'm witnessing is Jesus of Nazareth revealing Himself afresh through me to people around me. He does it with or without words. As Francis of Assisi declared, "Preach the Gospel at all times. Use words, when necessary."

15

Walking on Water

Anna Gimenez, Bishop John's sister, was a lovely lady, quietly elegant in her business suit, her hair always perfect. She had a twinkle in her eye that made one like her immediately, but she was self-effacing, always preferring someone else on the team do the presenting. Until the Spirit would come over her. Then she would speak with such quiet conviction authority that everyone who heard her was moved.

In mid-September, I called her in America For Jesus' new Washington, D.C. office. In the mornings she was usually in the office. In the afternoons and evenings she was usually out, meeting with different groups.

I asked her what was the most exciting thing, right now.

Watching God move. And knowing it's not yourself. It's nothing I do, because I don't know what I'm doing! It's pure grace! And it's going to stay with you, the rest of your life, because we've seen — we keep seeing — the impossible happen! And it's happening so fast!

The local Hispanic pastors are uniting! They called this morning. They're working with the press, radio, and television. They're putting it in the newspapers, sending out letters, announcing it on the radio every two hours and on television continually. You know, this started off as an event for just the Hispanics, *America Para Jesucristo*. And now — it's for everyone! As I told my brother a little while ago, we just didn't think God would do it!

He was doing it; there was no question about that.

Rallying the Hispanics has been my responsibility, right along. But now they're rallying themselves. In the newspaper, they're putting it as a convocation, saying that God has sounded the trumpet. They're going to blow the shofar, calling all the Hispanic pastors and leaders in the Metroplex area to a meeting three weeks before AFJ. And they're thorough. They're writing the pastors personal letters. They'll give them a week, and then they have staff ready to go call on all of them.

Pretty impressive. That kind of follow-up was going to produce results.

Listen to this: The man who is doing the newspaper advertising has also arranged to put our flyers in the five money-forwarding locations — you know, where Hispanics can go to send money to their families back in Latin America. And of course, these are the people we want — the ones who understand family obligations and who love God.

I didn't know what to say. Why had they grabbed on to it so? What exactly did she tell them?

Last night, one of the Hispanic pastors asked me, "What's the message of America For Jesus?" I said, "It's the same for you, as it is for the African-Americans, and for the Korean-Americans, and for all the Asian-Americans. God brought you here for such a time as this — to pray to save the nation!" That's what the Hispanic and African pastors have told me. They want to show their gratitude for this country, which all the way back sent missionaries all over the world, then took them in as refugees, and accepted them and loved them.

"This is the time," I tell them. "The time for us to stand with America. And pray for this country that we love and are so grateful to!"

Bottom line?

I warn them, this is no easy thing we've undertaken. This has cost my brother not only his health, but also his personal funds. He knows that God spared him for this, when he came back from his heart attack. We all know that. And the Lord has told me, some of us might have to die. Not physically, necessarily, but dying out to ourselves. But it's the time of the Lord. The awakening of the Church! We have to look at ourselves in repentance, without condemnation, that He might first heal the land in us — and then heal the land we live in.

All at once, she laughed.

I've told those Hispanic pastors that when we started, we were walking on water — pure faith. Now we're running on water! And I say, "Come with us! If you're right next to me, and we're running in the same direction, hold on! It's fun! When it's God calling you, the water is solid. You're running on rock!"

16

To Seek His Face

It was now five weeks to America For Jesus. Time for one last call to the one responsible for hearing God that put the whole thing in motion, Bishop John Gimenez. What did it look like now?

> Every day we receive fresh confirmation that God is sovereignly in charge, opening doors we never could have opened, moving on hearts we never could have reached. I spoke with Glenn Plummer this morning, chairman of the National Religious Broadcasters. He is with us and will be there. Also, Ted Haggard of the World Prayer Center called. He's coming, and he's telling everyone about it. Also, Steve Strang. Also, I got a call from Focus on the Family; the director of their Hispanic arm is on board. And that's just this morning.

Sounded like it was getting easier.

> It never gets easier. But the momentum is clearly building. You can feel it starting to roll across the nation. God is speaking into hearts, telling them to get involved, to come, to be part of the history He is going to make. In the last two weeks, you won't believe what will happen!

Actually, I might. I told him how one of the organizers of the Kansas City Charismatic Conference described that event. It was like getting a huge elephant moving. At first, you sat on it, poking and prodding it, wondering if it would ever get going. But once it got started, it began to gather momentum, going faster and faster, until finally it was crashing through the jungle, and you were holding onto its ears for dear life!

He laughed, and I asked him what was the most encouraging thing right now?

> God is doing it. All of it. All He needs is our obedience and our prayers. And speaking of prayer, we will have quite an undergirding — nonstop prayer on the Mall day and night, for the six days before the rally. Youth With A Mission is coming to be part of that, as are the young people in The Call, and intercessor groups from everywhere. In case it rains, there will be a tent to pray in, provided by The Justice Foundation.

What had it been like in the beginning?

> Much harder. The Church wasn't supporting it. No one was. Even my wife was reluctant to get on board. She had seen what it had taken out of me before — out of us, and our church — and she really did not want to see us go through that again. And when I had my heart attack, Pat Robertson, an old and dear friend, came to see me. "John," he said, concerned, "maybe you should stop trying to save the world."
>
> But I couldn't stop. That was what I felt God was saying to me through the heart attack. Don't hold back. Don't reject the expanded vision. He wanted everyone there, not just the Hispanics. The whole Church!

Back in 1980, we'd known the need was great, but it was nothing like it was now.

Satan wants to take this nation to the very depths of hell. And who's going to stop him? Only God. And He will only do it if we fulfill our part of the 2 Chronicles bargain. Righteousness exalts a nation. It must be the foundation of any call of God.

Righteousness — it was a long time coming.

It will come, if people repent. It's like the prodigal son, finally coming to his senses. We need to come to our senses, realize what bad shape we're in. When we see it, we'll be appalled. And we'll repent.

And then?

Righteousness — then faith — then reconciliation. Across the board. It's not enough for individuals to be reconciled. It must go way beyond that. Church and church. Denomination and denomination.

The trouble is, we all think we're right! If we're supposed to love our enemies, how much more are we to love our friends? The thing that has probably kept the church from the fullness of God, is that we have yet to learn how to love one another. It will only happen, when we come to that place of truly loving.

What exactly did he mean by *truly loving*?

First Corinthians 13 explains quite clearly what God considers love. It's not what we consider love. Our definition of love falls far short of His, because when we think of love, we usually want something. What God considers love is all about giving and considering others, and desiring good for them. Our interpretation is filled with I, me, mine. His is the opposite.

And that was what had to change, if we were to achieve restoration?

When we come to the place of truly loving one another, then full restoration of the sons of God will be given back to the Church. We talk about being sons of God, but let's be serious here: How often do we think of that church down the street as our enemy? That attitude is based on one word: self-ishness. I'm afraid that's pretty much where it's at for the Body of Christ in this country.

Nothing could change, until we came to a new under-standing of what it meant to love one another.

Righteousness and faith bring unity of purpose. And if we have unity of purpose, we will have vic-tory. There will be no victory without unity. Vic-tory always brings peace. When you have peace, then it's like the prodigal son has returned — then you rejoice.

And revival began.

Revival has to happen in the Church first, be-fore it can truly happen in the world around us. That's the purpose of America For Jesus: to bring us to that place of unity.

Many talk about righteousness and preach it, but righteousness demands sacrifice. And sacrifice means you give up something you don't want to give up.

What did he think was the hardest thing for people to give up?

> One of the hardest things we must give up in the pursuit of righteousness is *time*. Because we have all become so very busy! It's hard for us to give up time for unity. Our busyness has become almost the enemy of the Kingdom. It has become a religion. We think that all we're doing in the name of our ministry is of God.
>
> But God can't even get our attention! We're totally booked up — two, three, four years ahead of time! We are not hearing what the Spirit is saying to the Church. We are hearing what our ministry is saying to us. And thus, when Gods wants to bring His people into a state of unity, in order to affect the Church — or our nation — we tell God we can't be there. We're busy!

Ouch! That would cause some people to wince. Was it true of the prophets, too?

> Even the prophets are too busy! They must have an appointment to prophesy to one another!
>
> God is going to have to intervene once again, in such a way as to get the attention of the Church. The prophets of God are the watchmen on the wall. And as in the days of Nehemiah, there must be a trumpet sound, alerting us to the dangers that will ultimately destroy our home, our family, our nation, and our Church.
>
> Unless we wake up and realize that our house is on fire, we'll lose it all. It will all be destroyed. And who will be to blame? The watchmen whom God has set over the city.

And our only hope was…

Found in the book of 2 Chronicles, chapter 7, verse 14. God has the antidote to the poison Satan is using to destroy the nation. There is no other hope than the response of the people of God — no one else on the planet, no army, no government, no political party or religious entity to do it for us. Only those who are called by His name. If we will adhere to His plan, then will He forgive, and then will He heal.